The Story of AMERIGO VESPUCCI

FORGOTTEN VOYAGER

Ann Fitzpatrick Alper

Carolrhoda Books, Inc./Minneapolis

To Putnam Kennedy, M.D., whose efforts to tell Americans about Amerigo's achievements, so that we might understand our name, inspired this book.

Text copyright © 1991 by Ann Fitzpatrick Alper
All rights reserved. No part of this book may be reproduced, stored in a retrieval system, or transmitted in any form or by any means, electronic, mechanical, photocopying, recording, or otherwise, without the prior written permission of the Publisher except for the inclusion of brief quotations in an acknowledged review.

Library of Congress Cataloging-in-Publication Data

Alper, Ann Fitzpatrick.
    Forgotten voyager : the story of Amerigo Vespucci / Ann Fitzpatrick Alper.
        p. cm.
    Includes bibliographical references and index.
    ISBN 0-87614-442-3
    1. Vespucci, Amerigo, 1451-1512—Juvenile literature.
2. Explorers—America—Biography—Juvenile literature.
3. Explorers—Spain—Biography—Juvenile literature. 4. America—Discovery and exploration—Spanish—Juvenile literature.
I. Title.
E125.V5A62   1991
970.01'6'092—dc20
[B]   90-41242
                                                              CIP
                                                            rev. AC

Manufactured in the United States of America

    2   3   4   5   6   7   8   9   10   00   99   98   97   96   95   94   93   92

Contents

This fresco painting by the Italian painter Ghirlandaio is in the Ognissanti church in Florence, Italy. It contains portraits of the Vespucci family, including Amerigo (standing at left in the lower part of the painting).

I
City at the Crossroads

When Amerigo Vespucci was born in 1454, the wealthy city of Florence seemed the very center of the world to the people who lived there. Located in the north central part of the Italian peninsula, it sat on a trade route that stretched from the Indies in the Far East to England in the northwest. From his earliest days, Amerigo heard a great deal about these Indies. Gold, silk, and wonderful spices came from there. He learned that "the Indies" was what Europeans called the countries of the Far East.

Only a block from his house, Amerigo saw boats on the Arno River loaded with trade goods. Mules weighed down with goods clattered through the Ognissanti section of Florence, where the Vespuccis lived.

As he grew, Amerigo came to understand how important this trade was. Not only did Florentines enjoy the luxuries of the Indies themselves, but many of

Europeans brought many spices, such as cinnamon, ginger, and pepper, from the Indies to trade throughout Europe.

them also made their livings by trading the goods all over Europe.

Skilled Florentine dyers turned silk from China beautiful colors with dyes and alum that also came from the Indies. Then they sold the cloth to the English and other Europeans. Florentine artisans imported gold from the Indies and turned it into exquisite jewelry that was prized all over Europe. Plants from the East were used in making glass, soap, and medicines.

But even though all this trade took place, no one from Florence or any other part of Europe actually saw the Indies. The Muslim Turks who controlled the Middle East wouldn't let their old enemies, the

Christian Europeans, through their territory to the Far East.

The Christian Europeans thought Muslims were "heathens," which meant they were not God's people. Europeans had fought crusades to push the heathens from the land they controlled. The Turks had fought back fiercely. The year before Amerigo was born, the sultan of Turkey had captured Constantinople, the last Christian city in the Middle East, and now Europeans couldn't even go there. They had to pay terribly high prices to the sultan for the goods that came through his lands. Europeans badly wanted to find another route to the Indies—especially Florentines, because they relied on trade.

Amerigo, like other Italian boys, was undoubtedly fascinated by the tales of one European who had managed to see the Indies. Two hundred years earlier, Marco Polo, an Italian merchant, had gone all the way to China during a time when the Turks had not controlled the Middle East.

After 25 years of traveling, he came home and wrote about the richly dressed people he'd seen there, and about their marble bridges and luxurious palaces. Europeans thought if they could just find a way to these riches, they would become rich themselves.

Amerigo's father, Anastagio Vespucci, was a notary, and he worked for Lorenzo de' Medici, a very rich merchant who headed Florence's government. (Florence was a city-state, which ruled itself and belonged to no kingdom.)

Lorenzo de' Medici, known as Lorenzo the Magnificent, was the powerful ruler of the city-state of Florence.

There were other Vespuccis in Ognissanti as well. Their houses pressed up against each other in a tumble of stone balconies and turrets. Most of the Vespuccis were merchants dealing in wine or olive oil or wool. Some were bankers. Like other Florentines, they loved art and learning, poetry and music.

Anastagio Vespucci was interested in geography and astronomy as well as business. He also enjoyed reading ancient Greek and Roman authors. The Greeks and Romans had known more than the people who lived after them, he told Amerigo. It was the Florentines who named the eight hundred years after the fall of the Roman empire the "Dark Ages." During these Dark Ages, people did not value learning and forgot much that the Romans and Greeks had known. Now the people of Florence were rediscovering this ancient knowledge. These years of rediscovery were later called the Renaissance (which means rebirth).

Anastagio Vespucci and his brother Giorgio, a teacher and Dominican monk, got excited whenever they heard news of a Roman statue being dug up somewhere. They pooled their money and bought old documents and maps. They studied Greek astronomy.

Amerigo's mother, Elisabetta, was quite different. Like most women of Florence, she'd been given no schooling, and frowned when Amerigo asked questions. Besides, she favored her oldest son, Antonio. From the time Amerigo was small, he knew the oldest brother in a Florentine family was special. It was the oldest son who inherited most of the family wealth and his father's title or position.

When he was six, Amerigo joined Antonio and Girolamo, the second brother, in studying with Father Umberto, a priest who came to the house. The priest taught the boys reading, writing, arithmetic, and religion. Antonio would go to the University of Pisa after he learned the basics from the priest, but it was the custom to put third sons to work as soon as they could read, write, and figure. Amerigo was luckier than most third sons, however. He had a father who wanted all his boys to learn as much as they could. Amerigo would be given a special opportunity.

II
School Days

Anastagio Vespucci sent Amerigo to the Monastery of San Marco to study with his uncle Giorgio. Giorgio was a famous teacher, and Amerigo's classmates were not only other Italians, but boys from other parts of Europe as well. One student came all the way from Constantinople.

The boys studied Latin, the language of ancient Rome, along with math, grammar, history, Italian and Greek literature, geography, and astronomy. Amerigo was fascinated with astronomy. The stars formed patterns in the sky like pictures. Uncle Giorgio called the patterns constellations, and Amerigo learned to recognize them all.

Studying maps was interesting too. When Amerigo first came to the school, Uncle Giorgio showed him a world map he said was the one that boys in other parts of Europe studied. It showed the seas and the three continents of the world—Asia (where the Indies were), Africa, and Europe.

Near the top of the map were Adam and Eve in the Garden of Eden. On one side was a picture of the devil gathering his forces to invade the Christian world. On the other side were a castle and strange animals representing the kingdom of Prester John.

Most Europeans had heard of this kingdom. Three hundred years before, a letter had gone around Europe. It was supposed to have come from Prester John, allegedly a great Christian king who, it was said, ruled wisely over a land somewhere in the Far East. The letter told of strange people there. Some were horses from the waist down, it said. Some had one eye in front and three or four in the back of their heads. There were creatures in the kingdom called griffins— birds big enough to carry horses to their nests.

Over the centuries, as the letter was recopied, the kingdom of Prester John grew even more fantastic. It told of wonders such as underground rivers that turned into precious stones. Europeans believed these tales and dreamed of finding the kingdom.

Uncle Giorgio showed Amerigo another map and told him to look at the difference between it and the first one. There were no pictures on the second map—just the seas, the three continents of the world, and straight lines going from top to bottom and side to side on top of them. It was the world map made by Paolo Toscanelli. The map was based on the work of Ptolemy, an ancient Greek geographer who, twelve

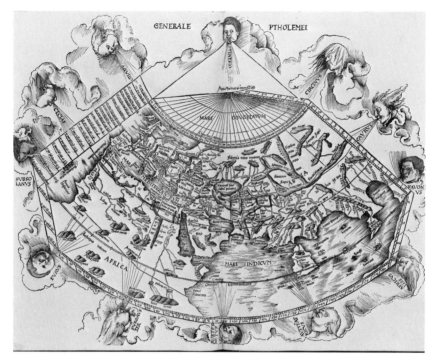

This map of the world is an illustration from a Latin translation of Ptolemy's *Geography*, published in 1511.

hundred years before, had figured out that the world was round. Ptolemy divided the earth into halves called hemispheres. The line between the northern and southern hemispheres he called the equator.

Like most boys of the time, Amerigo probably wanted to travel the world and see what it was really like. But in his first year at San Marco, Amerigo discovered that might not be so easy. Europeans couldn't go east to Asia, where the Indies were, because of the Turks. They couldn't go very far south into Africa, either, because they were afraid of being burned to a crisp when they neared the equator. The ancient Greeks

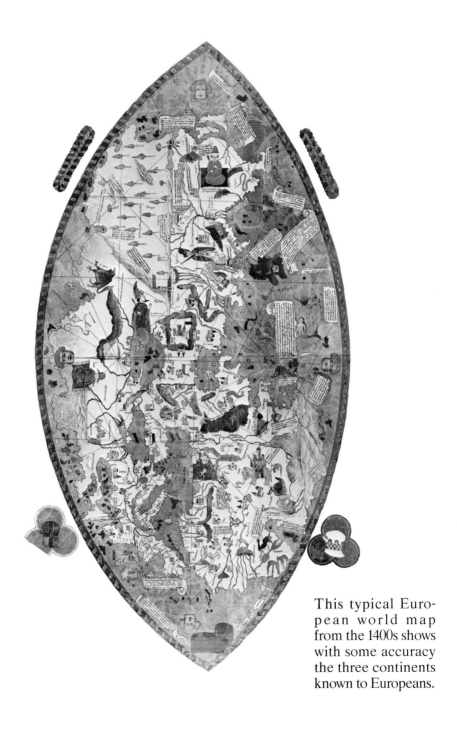

This typical European world map from the 1400s shows with some accuracy the three continents known to Europeans.

and Romans said the equator was a ring of fire, and the seas boiled there. Flames shot down from the sky. Although Europeans sometimes went to Egypt and Morocco in North Africa, they stayed well north of the equator.

West of Europe, Amerigo learned, was the great Ocean Sea, the body of water now called the Atlantic Ocean. Sailors were afraid of its unknown winds and currents. Many still believed it was full of monsters that could eat a ship in a single bite. And north of Europe, the land was covered with ice.

In school, Amerigo learned about Prince Henry of Portugal, called Henry the Navigator, who had pushed his sailors to sail farther and farther south along the coast of Africa toward the equator. Arab caravans were bringing gold to Europe from somewhere in Africa, and Henry wanted to find out where. He also thought the kingdom of Prester John might be in Africa.

Henry died when Amerigo was little, but the king of Portugal was continuing his work. Even though the king tried to keep his expeditions a secret from other countries, the Florentines knew about them. There were Florentine bankers in Portugal, and the geographer Toscanelli had friends there. Toscanelli wrote the Portuguese king suggesting it would be easier to find the gold of the Indies by sailing west across the Ocean Sea. He sent a nautical map of the sea and the lands around it to the king.

Toscanelli's idea seemed too risky to the Portuguese king, however. He kept sending his expeditions down the coast of Africa. They always stopped a good deal short of the equator. The Portuguese sailors were afraid they wouldn't be able to turn around and sail against the southerly coastal currents when they needed to escape the equator's heat and flames.

Then news came to Florence of new ships, called caravels, that the Portuguese were building. They were narrower and lighter than the round-bellied carracks then in use. The caravels were only about 20 feet across the beam and 60 or 70 feet long.

The Portuguese had learned to rig the caravels so they sailed very well against the wind and currents. The Florentine scholars said it was only a matter of time before the Portuguese saw the equator.

Amerigo was lucky to be listening to the best minds in Europe, instead of working like most younger sons his age. By now, Amerigo knew the best minds in Florence were the best minds in Europe.

He was 19 when the Portuguese finally sailed all the way to the equator. They found no boiling seas there, and no flames shot down from the sky. There was just a coastline like the coastline farther north. It must have surprised Amerigo to learn that even Greek ideas could be wrong.

As Amerigo grew more mature, he gradually realized he had little chance of seeing the world. Florence was only a city-state, not a nation like Portugal. It had merchant ships but no real navy of its own. Instead of traveling, he would study as long as possible and then go into business in Florence.

III
In France and Spain

When Amerigo was 24, another of his father's brothers, Guido, made him an unexpected offer. Conspirators had tried to kill Lorenzo de' Medici, Florence's ruler, because they were jealous of his power. They had failed, but were planning to try again with the help of the Pope's army and the army of the king of Naples. Lorenzo was sending Guido, a diplomat and businessman, to Paris to get help from the French king. Guido wanted Amerigo to come along as his assistant and secretary.

The opportunity to go to a faraway place like Paris was an unusual one for a third son. Amerigo accepted Guido's offer, and they set out immediately. They probably traveled with guards, as robbers often attacked people on the roads and killed them for their money and property.

On the way, Amerigo and Guido stopped in other

Italian city-states and duchies. Amerigo wrote to Lorenzo telling him which ones were willing to help him fight off the conspirators.

King Louis XI was away when Guido and Amerigo finally arrived in Paris, but they used their time to meet with French nobles and gain their support. When the king returned, Guido got a pledge of help from him, and Amerigo immediately sent home the news. Then he and Guido left Paris.

They didn't go right home, however. They stopped in several cities to do business for Lorenzo. Amerigo learned about wool trading and how to sell wheat at the highest prices as well as the details of the wine and olive oil trade. He even learned banking. By the time they reached Florence, over two years had passed. It was 1481, and Amerigo had turned 27.

He was shocked to see how old his father looked. Soon after Amerigo's return, Anastagio died. Fortunately, as soon as Amerigo finished settling his father's business affairs, Lorenzo de' Medici offered him a job.

Amerigo accepted and went to work as a clerk and secretary. His work earned Amerigo a living, but he was glad when Lorenzo's cousin, also named Lorenzo, offered him a job that would use more of the skills he learned from Uncle Guido. This Lorenzo was called "Il Popolano," which means "man of the people." He wanted Amerigo to run his household and several of his businesses.

While working for Il Popolano, Amerigo became

Amerigo accompanied his uncle Guido Vespucci on a trip to Paris on behalf of Lorenzo de' Medici.

close to his brother Antonio's son, Giovanni. Giovanni was interested in the stars and maps and liked to spend time with his uncle Amerigo, just as Amerigo had spent time with Giorgio and Guido.

Early in 1489, Florentines heard news that a Portuguese ship had finally sailed around the southern tip of Africa. Now all they had to do was sail east to reach the Indies. Everyone in Florence talked of the great achievement. The Portuguese king, people said, would probably never heed Toscanelli's advice to sail west now.

In September of that same year, Amerigo got a chance to go on a trip of his own. Il Popolano wanted him to go to the Spanish city of Seville to meet with a man named Gianetto Berardi. Amerigo was to see if Berardi would be a good person to take over the management of Il Popolano's businesses in Seville.

A trip to Spain wasn't like sailing around Africa or across the Ocean Sea, but Amerigo would be seeing new places and learning to speak a new language — and this time he would be on his own.

Seville turned out to be a captivating city. It was so foreign looking. The Moors had swept across North Africa from the Middle East eight hundred years earlier and conquered southern Spain. Though the Spanish had won the city back two hundred years before Amerigo arrived, he could see signs of the Middle East everywhere — in the olive-skinned people, in the songs, the tambourines, the delicate wrought iron and painted tiles of the courtyards. Even the cathedral had once been a mosque where Muslims worshipped.

And Seville felt like a port city. It wasn't on the Ocean Sea, but its river, the Guadalquivir, emptied into the sea not far away. Triana, across the river, was like a seaport, full of sailors and ship outfitters. A man could learn to be anything from cabin boy to captain just by spending time in the taverns and listening to the talk.

When Amerigo arrived, most of the talk was of the recent agreement with Portugal, which allowed the Spanish to go to Guinea in North Africa to bring home gold from newly discovered mines there. The Spanish were getting ready to push the Muslim Moors entirely out of Spain, and they needed gold to pay their army. Seville bustled with soldiers and the excitement of the coming battles. The Spanish also talked excitedly of Portugal's voyage around the tip of Africa.

Amerigo met with Berardi, who turned out to be friendly and kind. He seemed trustworthy as well, so Amerigo recommended him to Il Popolano. Amerigo also got acquainted with some of the other Italians living in Seville. There were Florentine bankers there, and Amerigo's brother Antonio was their notary in Florence. No one knows if Amerigo met Christopher Columbus at this time, but Columbus was there and knew Berardi. He and Amerigo were almost the same age. It is likely that they met then.

Columbus was from Genoa (in what is now Italy) and had spent much time in Lisbon, Portugal, trying to persuade the Portuguese king to give him ships and provisions for a voyage west across the Ocean Sea

SEVILIA.

This map of Seville, Spain, and its river, the Guadalquivir, appeared in a German geography book published in the late 1500s.

to the Indies. While there, he got a look at Toscanelli's map and letter to the king. They confirmed what he already thought. A trip west across the sea would certainly bring him to China or Cipangu (Japan). But since the Portuguese were now so close to having an eastern route to the Indies, Columbus had come to Seville to try to get Spanish backing for his plan to go west.

Amerigo heard people laugh at Columbus's idea and call it crazy, but he didn't think it was. Columbus was wise enough to have obtained a copy of the map that Toscanelli had sent the Portuguese king, and he was a master pilot (as navigators were then called).

When his work was done, Amerigo returned to Florence. He worked for Il Popolano for two more years there. Not much is known about this time.

The great Floren-
tine painter Sandro
Botticelli, who was
a close friend of the
Vespucci family,
painted this portrait
of Amerigo as a young
man.

Amerigo probably saw his childhood friend from
Ognissanti, Sandro Botticelli, now a famous painter.
Botticelli was busy decorating Florence's gigantic
cathedral. Amerigo's school friend Piero Soderini was
a member of the Signoria (city council). Amerigo's
brother Antonio was a successful notary with a wife
and family. Amerigo had a close relationship with
Antonio and spent time with his son Giovanni.

When Il Popolano needed to send him back to Seville
in 1491, Amerigo asked if he could stay there and
work for a while. As soon as Il Popolano said yes,
Amerigo left, taking Giovanni with him.

When they arrived in Seville, Berardi invited them

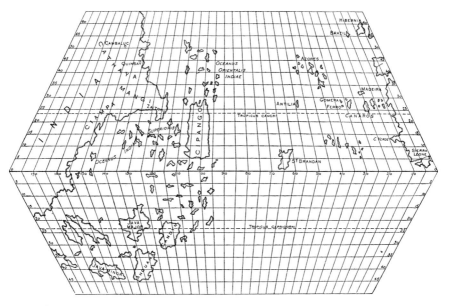

The famous map made by Florentine geographer Paolo Toscanelli in 1474 showed the Indies to the west of Europe. Columbus's determination to find a western route to the Indies was based in part on his knowledge of this map.

to live in his house. Amerigo felt at home there. The other Italians of Seville visited often, and they were all talking about Columbus. The Spanish queen and king, Isabella and Ferdinand, had finally consented to back his voyage across the Ocean Sea to the Indies. Then Amerigo heard that the king and queen couldn't give Columbus all the money he needed.

Amerigo, well educated in geography by Toscanelli and Uncle Giorgio, probably spoke to Berardi and the other Italians about his confidence in Columbus's plan. He could have told them about Toscanelli's map.

In any case, Berardi ended up lending Columbus a large sum of money. Rich Spaniards and the other

Italians of Seville lent Columbus the rest of the money he needed, and the explorer began preparations for the great adventure.

For several months, Columbus shuttled back and forth between the small port of Palos, on the Ocean Sea, and Triana, where he was gathering what he needed for his voyage. Columbus often stayed at Berardi's house, and Amerigo must have heard a lot about his methods of navigation.

One navigation tool Columbus was using was the quadrant. The quadrant was a quarter-circle of metal with a pair of sighting holes on one of its straight edges. A string with a weight on one end was attached. When the quadrant was held up so that the Pole Star (the North Star) could be seen through both sighting holes, the weighted string would fall across the curved edge of the quadrant where degrees were marked. All a pilot had to do was read off the figure to know how many degrees above the equator or south of the North Pole he was. This position was called latitude.

Amerigo knew about another navigational instrument called a mariner's astrolabe, which not only told latitude but gave information about the position of the stars. Columbus wasn't using an astrolabe, though. He was sailing across the Ocean Sea with only a quadrant, a compass, and his own experienced eye to guide him.

At last Columbus's ships, the *Niña*, the *Pinta*, and the *Santa María*, were ready to sail. Before dawn on August 3, 1492, they hauled up their anchors and floated out with the ebb tide.

Those who watched were frightened to see ships embark upon a sea whose winds and currents were unknown. But they were excited too. Columbus might see the Chinese emperor, just as Marco Polo had met the great Kublai Khan two hundred years before. He might see the Forbidden City and Chinese grandees dressed in cloth of gold and jewels. Maybe he'd see the emperor traveling in a room attached to the backs of four elephants as Marco Polo had.

There was no wind, and the ships were visible for hours. Finally they disappeared over the western horizon.

IV
Amerigo the Navigator

After several months had passed and no one had heard from Columbus, people began to wonder if he were shipwrecked. Columbus had said the *Santa María* was "a dull sailor unfit for discovery." What if he were stuck in the great sea of mud that many people were sure lay between Spain and Asia?

Then, seven months after he left, news came to Seville of Columbus's return to Palos. The clumsy *Santa María* was wrecked, but the caravels, the *Niña* and the *Pinta*, had brought the explorers home. Columbus had discovered an island that he said was just off the coast of China and called it Hispaniola. (The island was actually near Cuba and consists of what are now Haiti and Santo Domingo.) The explorer had even started a colony on Hispaniola with the sailors from the wrecked *Santa María*.

When Columbus and his crew reached Seville, they

paraded through the streets with ten bronze-skinned men they called "Indians." (Columbus believed he had been in the Indies and therefore called the native people Indians.) The Indians carried cages enclosing red and green parrots such as had never been seen in Europe. The explorers held up nuggets of gold. How different the Indians were from what Amerigo had been led to expect. Why weren't they wearing the cloth of gold and jewels that Marco Polo had described?

Columbus had to leave for Barcelona to see the king and queen. He wanted to take all the Indians, but four of them were feeling sick. He left them with Amerigo and Berardi while he went to the royal court. Columbus, like other Christians of his time, believed that "heathen" were not people of God and thus were scarcely human. Making slaves of them, therefore, seemed perfectly all right.

Soon good news from Barcelona reached Seville. The king and queen had made Columbus Admiral of the Ocean Sea and viceroy of the newly discovered lands. And they said he alone would be in charge of further exploration of the Indies.

When Columbus returned to Seville, he told Amerigo and Berardi he had a job for them. King Ferdinand was sending him back to Hispaniola, and the king wanted Amerigo and Berardi to be in charge of outfitting 17 ships for this second voyage. King Ferdinand was afraid the Portuguese would try to take over Hispaniola or lands nearby and wanted Columbus to start a Spanish colony there. The queen wanted the natives taught the Christian religion, for, like other Europeans of the time, she felt it her duty to convert the "heathen."

For four months, Amerigo and Berardi had little time for anything but looking after Columbus's needs. They signed on crews, chartered ships, armed them with cannon, supplied lances, swords, sea biscuit, wine, flour, oil, vinegar, and cheese. They helped find masons, carpenters, smiths, workmen, and farmers for the colony, as well as tools and seeds. The queen wanted a church built, so Amerigo and Berardi even had to find priests to go to the colony.

Finally, on September 25, 1493, Columbus sailed on his second voyage. But Amerigo and Berardi still didn't rest. The king put them to work outfitting more ships to go to Hispaniola. The ships would resupply Columbus and bring home the wealth he found in the Indies. The offices of Amerigo and Berardi became the place people went when they wanted to know anything about Columbus or his colony.

When the first ships came back from the new colony, some disturbing news came with them. Columbus was a harsh and unjust governor, people were saying. Columbus hadn't found anything but pretty feathers and a few bits of gold, not the wealth described by Marco Polo. Columbus had made everyone swear that Cuba was part of a mainland and not an island, even though no one knew for sure.

These reports, along with pressure from would-be

Upon his return to Spain after his first voyage to Hispaniola, Columbus was summoned to the court of King Ferdinand and Queen Isabella to explain his explorations to them.

explorers, caused the king to break his promise to Columbus that only he would explore the Indies. Now Ferdinand issued a royal edict saying that any Spaniard who wished to sail to the Indies might do so.

Only Hispaniola would be reserved for Columbus to explore.

Amerigo and Berardi assembled a fleet of 12 more supply ships to go out to Columbus. They worked as fast as they could, hoping the supplies would make the colonists more content with their situation and with Columbus. Then Berardi fell ill, and Amerigo had to do most of the work. He ran back and forth to Triana, signing up pilots and crews. He charted the route with the pilots, and got information on the sea and the islands from people returning from Hispaniola. While still on dry land, Amerigo was becoming a sailor.

Then, on December 15, 1495, Berardi died, leaving Amerigo in charge of everything. Amerigo was saddened by Berardi's death, but he went on supplying the king's ships. He also realized he wanted to get married to a young woman he had met, Maria Cerezo. At 41 years of age, Amerigo became engaged.

In June of 1496, Columbus returned from his second voyage, looking like a pitiful old man. He felt disgraced by the tales the settlers had sent to the king and queen. He told his side to anyone who would listen. When he had arrived in Hispaniola, he found all the colonists from the wrecked Santa Maria had been killed in battles with Indians. He established a new colony on the island, then left for other lands. He had to find the riches he'd promised the king and queen.

He had found little gold, and when he had returned to Hispaniola, his new settlers were shaking with fever and pale with hunger. When he had heard about the complaints they were sending back to King Ferdinand and Queen Isabella on the royal supply ships, Columbus had decided to come home and defend his reputation.

While waiting for the king and queen to see him, Columbus told people in Seville that the colonists were disobedient. He was viceroy, and they should do what he told them to do. All they wanted was to get rich, not to be loyal subjects. The king and queen took four months before they allowed the explorer to come to court in October of 1496 and tell them this.

No one really knows for sure what happened next to Amerigo, but the following May he may have sailed across the Ocean Sea himself. Exactly where the voyage took him is uncertain, but some historians now feel the ships touched land somewhere in Central America and sailed north for several months, reaching what is now known as Cape Hatteras in North Carolina.

Whether he went on the voyage for the king or as a private citizen is unknown, but businessmen were backing voyages in hopes of finding riches and making a profit. Amerigo's voyage may have been sponsored by Italian bankers. He was probably included among the sailors because of the knowledge he'd gained planning voyages for others and because he knew astronomy, a great help in navigation.

In any case, it is known that Amerigo was back in Seville by October of 1498 and married Maria Cerezo. Now he had a family—his wife, and his nephew Giovanni, who was like a son to him. He learned that Columbus had left on his third voyage, and the news

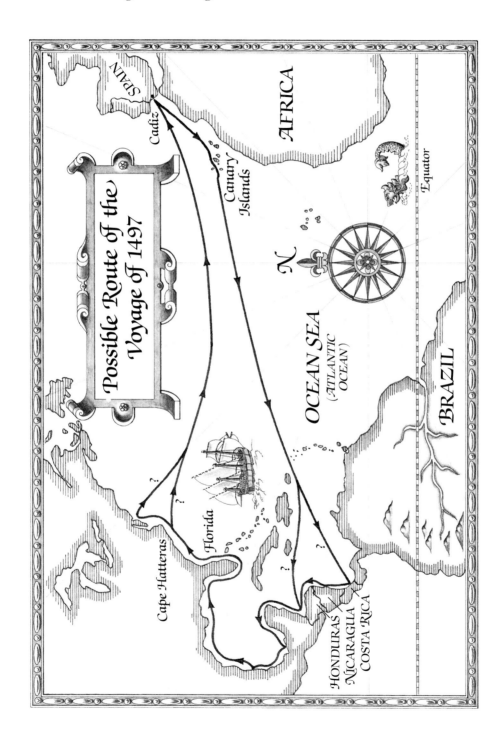

Possible Route of the
Voyage of 1497

SPAIN

Cadiz

Canary
Islands

AFRICA

Equator

N

OCEAN SEA
(ATLANTIC
OCEAN)

BRAZIL

Cape Hatteras

Florida

HONDURAS
NICARAGUA
COSTA RICA

that was coming back to Spain from Hispaniola was worse than before. The people didn't want Columbus to govern them. They had rebelled against him.

Amerigo was summoned to court to see the king and queen. When he got there, the king told him about the confusing reports he was getting from Hispaniola. Columbus was telling him one thing and the colonists another. The king didn't know what to believe. He wanted to find out the truth, and he wanted the Indies explored more thoroughly. He was sending out a four-ship expedition. Captain Alonso de Ojeda and pilot Juan de la Cosa would take two ships to Hispaniola. The other two ships would go farther south and explore. The king asked Amerigo to go as a pilot on one of the ships of exploration.

On May 16, 1499, Amerigo stood on the deck of a three-masted ship in the port of Cádiz. Salt breezes filled his nostrils and ruffled the hair around his ears. The sailors untied the heavy rope that bound the ship to the dock and heaved it on deck.

V

Under New Heavens

The expedition sailed south for a while down the coast of North Africa. Amerigo must have been excited to be seeing the same sights the Portuguese had seen so many times as they inched toward the equator. And there was a lot for his inquisitive eyes to take in as well—the way the sailors scrambled up the masts and the way the wind filled the ship's sails. The way the cabin boy turned the hourglass every half-hour and called out the time.

It was hard to use navigational instruments like the quadrant or astrolabe to figure latitude on board ship. Measuring the angle of the sun to the horizon was one way of telling, but the deck moved beneath Amerigo's feet and made the horizon seem to move. Gradually Amerigo found his "sea legs" and managed to tell the ship's latitude each day.

The explorers sailed down the coast of North

Africa until they reached a place 28 degrees north of the equator. Then they turned west toward the Canary Islands, which lay about 300 miles offshore. They sailed southwest around the Canaries to the Cape Verde Islands. Stopping at one called Fire Island, they took on fresh water and wood. Several days went by before the ships were provisioned. Finally everything was ready. Ojeda and de la Cosa set their course due west for the area of Hispaniola. The ship Amerigo was on and one other headed southwest to explore new territory.

Now they were alone in seas no European had traveled. Each day, the captain tried to figure out how far they'd gone by estimating how fast the ship was sailing. He told the sailor with the strongest arm to toss a log of wood out to sea in front of the ship. Then, as the bow (the front) of the ship came even with the log, the captain started counting. When the stern (the rear) of the ship passed the log, he stopped counting. The lower the number, the faster the ship was sailing. He wrote down the number of miles they'd gone every day "by the log." (Ships' daily records are still called logs.)

Sometimes the captain had a sailor attach a rope to the log before he threw it out to sea. The rope had knots in it 50 feet apart. The captain turned a minute glass over and counted the number of knots the ship passed during the time it took the sand to run to the bottom of the glass. If they passed four, he said they were doing four knots. (Sailors still

In the 1400s and 1500s, many Europeans still believed that the Atlantic Ocean was filled with monsters and strange creatures. This 16th century engraving shows Vespucci sailing across the perilous ocean.

measure speed and distances in knots.) Columbus's method was to count his own heartbeats during the time it took his ship to pass a log.

Amerigo was supposed to share a cabin with the other pilots, but at night he dragged his straw-filled mattress out on deck to watch the stars. The farther south the ships went, the more unfamiliar constellations he saw. He made a map of the heavens, adding new stars as they appeared. Amerigo wanted to be the first European to see the "south star." He wrote that perhaps his name would live after him in history if he did.

After three weeks of sailing before a steady wind, the men began to wonder when they would see land. Amerigo wished he could figure out exactly how far west they'd gone. At night he watched the sky, trying to think of some way the stars could help.

A few days later, a sailor sighted land. Amerigo peered westward and saw a line of green shimmering against the horizon. As the ship got closer, he saw that the green was a solid line of trees. Amerigo and the sailors gave thanks to God and then lowered rowboats to explore.

Amerigo's quadrant told him the ships had landed four degrees north of the equator. Since Amerigo believed each degree represented 16 2/3 leagues, he thought he was about 67 leagues (or about 200 miles) away from it. He was in what is now Brazil, and it wasn't nearly as hot as Europeans thought equatorial lands must be. Amerigo later wrote about how green the trees were and how good they smelled. Many were over 200 feet tall, with trunks more than 3 feet thick. Others were shorter and full of colored flowers.

The explorers rowed their boats up to the trees, but they grew so thickly, no one could find a place to get out of the rowboats. They went north looking for a spot, then turned south. All day they tried to land, but the trees seemed to grow right out of the water.

Finally, they gave up and returned to the ships. The Cape of Catigara was supposed to be eight degrees south of the equator. According to Ptolemy's map, sailing around the cape would put them near the country in Asia called India. They could look for a place to land as they sailed toward Catigara.

South they went, and for the next few days, Amerigo stood on deck watching the green shoreline slip past, enjoying the soft breezes, and looking for signs of Marco Polo's Asia. He wished the ships could sail closer to land, but the captain was afraid of running aground in the shallow coastal waters.

Every day at noon, Amerigo watched the sun cast its shadow on the deck. Each day the shadow grew smaller. Finally it cast no noonday shadow at all. That meant they'd reached the equator—and were the first Europeans to do so on this side of the Ocean Sea.

The expedition kept sailing south until they came to a place where the seawater tasted fresh rather than salty, even though they were miles out to sea. Venturing closer to shore, the explorers saw a huge river pouring its water into the sea. A river so huge couldn't come from an island, so they must have reached China. But where were the cities of gold and marble and the richly dressed people?

The explorers put provisions for four days into the rowboats, strapped on their swords, and rowed toward shore. When they entered the river mouth, they found two rivers flowing into it. The explorers decided to

The densely forested coastline of Brazil must have surprised Amerigo and his fellow sailors, who were expecting to find the cities and palaces that Marco Polo had described.

row up the larger of the two (which is now called the Amazon).

They paddled for miles looking for a place to land. Amerigo was astonished by the birds he saw among the trees. Later he wrote to Il Popolano, "Some were crimson colored, others of . . . green and lemon, others entirely green and others . . . were black and flesh-colored." Their songs were so sweet, Amerigo wrote, "that we often lingered, listening to their lovely music."

The seamen rowed farther and farther inland. "We attempted to land in many places . . ." Amerigo wrote later, "but found the low land . . . so thickly covered with trees that the birds could scarcely fly through them." After two days of exploring, the men gave up and turned the boats around.

They reboarded the ships and went south, still hoping to reach Ptolemy's Cape of Catigara. They sailed to six degrees south of the equator without finding a place to land. Then a fierce northerly current made progress almost impossible. The captains put up all the sails to catch the wind blowing south but still couldn't sail against the current. It tore at the ships' hulls and threatened to sink them. Finally they gave up and turned around.

Amerigo was disappointed. He believed he was in the Indies and longed to reach Catigara, which, according to Ptolemy's map, was just about a hundred miles away. Watching the stars finally took his mind off his disappointment. He wrote Il Popolano that he was thrilled to be sailing "between the two poles, within sight of two heavens. I lost my sleep many nights contemplating the movement of the stars of the other pole."

Amerigo had an almanac with him that showed the position of the moon and planets each hour of the night for every night of the year. It was mid-August, and he noticed the almanac said that the moon and Mars would appear to be in the same place in the sky, or in conjunction, in the city of Ferrara (in what is now Italy) at midnight on August 23. On the evening of the twenty-third, Amerigo noted the moon and Mars met not at midnight but at 5:30 in the evening when observed from where he was. That meant when it was midnight in Ferrara, it was 5:30 in the evening on his side of the Ocean Sea. There was a difference of 6½ hours.

Suddenly Amerigo realized he could now figure out his distance from Ferrara in miles. Ptolemy had written that the earth was close to 24,000 miles in circumference. Amerigo knew it turned all the way around every 24 hours. That meant it turned almost 1,000 miles an hour, so 6½ hours equalled almost 6,500 miles. Amerigo made some more calculations, using Ptolemy's exact figure for the circumference of the earth, and figured his distance east of Ferrara. Then he calculated his distance east of Cádiz, Spain, the port from which he'd sailed. He knew how far west he'd gone. He knew his longitude.

Now, if sailors carried almanacs that told when stars and the moon crossed paths in European cities, they could observe what time the same conjunction took place where they were. When they figured the difference in time, they'd know their approximate difference in miles. Using Ptolemy's exact figure, they could then calculate their exact longitude.

Every night, Amerigo watched the stars and made his calculations. Now that he knew his position east and west as well as north and south, he could map the coastline correctly. Latitude lines going from side to side were already on Amerigo's map. Now he could draw lines of longitude from top to bottom and put in the capes, inlets, rivers, and bays of the coast as they sailed. The sailors gave the places descriptive names in Spanish that meant "mudbanks," "overflowed land," "river of trees," "black mountain." They went north for hundreds of miles.

Ten degrees above the equator, they came to an island 46 miles off the coast. There was a beach where they could land. On it stood naked, black-haired people who were staring at the explorers.

Most Europeans still believed no one could live in the "torrid zone" near the equator, but here were people—and they were tan-skinned. Columbus believed people could live near the equator but thought the sun scorched their blood and turned them black. "Experience is certainly worth more than belief," Amerigo wrote to Il Popolano. Trusting his own eyes rather than accepting the myths of the day was Amerigo's guiding principle.

Amerigo and 21 others armed themselves and rowed ashore. The people received them in a friendly way, Amerigo wrote. "They took us to their houses, where they had very good food prepared. They gave us wine to drink made not of grapes but of other fruit. It was very good." The people gave the explorers other kinds of fruit to eat, and Amerigo found these delicious too. "They gave everything we asked of them but more, I think, through fear than affection." (He was probably describing the Carib people.)

Using sign language, the people told of their

The European explorers' first impressions of American "Indians" are reflected in this woodcut, made about 1505.

customs. It was their practice to eat prisoners they took in war. They said it made their enemies more afraid of them. Even though the European explorers thought nothing of killing "heathens" or making them slaves, they were shocked at this practice. The people seemed so friendly. They showed the explorers their bows, arrows, shields, and the canoes they used. And they gave the explorers pearls. The people said if the explorers stayed a few more days, they would go fishing and get more for them.

Not wanting to delay, Amerigo and the explorers left "with many parrots of various colors and friendly feelings." The ships continued northwestward along the coast, seeing many more people and animals. As they continued, the people who stood on shore looked less friendly. (These people were probably also Caribs, in what is now Venezuela.) They stood armed with bows and arrows held ready to fight. The explorers sailed on without stopping.

VI
Strange Shores

The coastline of Venezuela turned west, and the explorers followed it. They saw more naked people, probably of the Arawak tribe. Sometimes the explorers went ashore and traded with the local people. They had brought little bells and mirrors to give the Indians in exchange for bits of gold or other valuables.

The expedition went farther north and came to a gulf where another great river turned the seawater fresh. Here the people had pearls, and the explorers traded bells and mirrors for them. Since pearls had always come to Europe from the Indies, Amerigo still thought he must be sailing the coast of Asia.

As they went farther up the coast, Amerigo noticed the native people seemed more hostile. "We began to find people who did not wish for our friendship, but stood waiting for us with their . . . bows and arrows. . . ." One day, when the explorers tried to land on a beach, the people (probably Caribs) shot their arrows at them.

The explorers jumped out of their boats and fought back with swords, but so many Indians came at them, they finally turned and ran. According to Amerigo, one of the old sailors who'd stayed to guard the boats called out to them, "Boys, boys, turn your faces to your enemies and God will give you victory!" "Throwing himself on his knees, he prayed, and then rushed furiously at the Indians," Amerigo wrote. "We all joined with him, wounded as we were . . . we routed them and killed 150. We burned their houses also . . . ."

In those days, Europeans felt they had God's blessing to destroy the property of non-Christians and even to kill them. Amerigo, though more enlightened than most, was no exception. Like Columbus, he enslaved or killed many of the people whose lands he explored.

Many seamen were wounded, and the ships had to stay offshore until the sailors' wounds healed. One of the sailors died. After 20 days, the expedition set sail again and finally landed on an island (now called Curaçao). Amerigo was amazed at its people. "Each one was taller when upon his knees than I when standing erect." Marco Polo hadn't written anything about such tall people. Amerigo must have wondered where he was.

After many more miles of sailing off the coast of the country now called Venezuela, Amerigo saw an island (probably Aruba) with a village of houses built

SPAIN

Cadiz

AFRICA

The Second Voyage
1499–1500

Hispaniola

Cape Verde
Islands

VESPUCCI

OJEDA

VENEZUELA

Equator

Cape São Roque

BRAZIL

Cape São Agustin

OCEAN
SEA

N

on stilts over the sea. It reminded him of the Italian city of Venice which was built over water. The explorers called the village Venezuela, which means "Little Venice."

When they rowed ashore, the people shot arrows at them. The sailors raised their shields and fought back. Finally the Indians fled, and the explorers entered the empty village. They found that the houses were filled with finely woven cotton cloth and skillfully constructed with beams made of Brazil wood.

As the ships continued up the coast, Amerigo counted the different languages the people spoke. In those days, Europeans believed there were not more than 77 languages spoken in the world. "I say there are more than 1,000," Amerigo wrote. "I have heard more than 40 myself."

They kept sailing north until they came to the latitude of Hispaniola. The men were tired, and the ships' hulls eaten by worms, so they turned east and sailed to Columbus's colony. There they rested for two months.

Then they sailed north once more, possibly all the way to the Bahamas. By this time, food was scarce. The men were down to six ounces of bread a day and three measures of water. They took on supplies, then captured some of the "heathen" to sell as slaves and headed home.

The expedition reached the port of Cádiz in Spain on June 8, 1500, 13 months after leaving it. Amerigo hurried home to Seville but, when he got there, came down with a fever. Maria didn't know what was wrong with him, but she took care of him as well as she could. (Historians think Amerigo caught malaria on the swampy coasts he explored).

As soon as he felt better, Amerigo made a globe of the world for the king and queen and took it to them in Granada. Ferdinand and Isabella were pleased with the globe and the 14 flesh-colored pearls Amerigo laid before the queen. But they were more excited by the information that he'd sailed two thousand miles along one coast. The length of his journey proved the land was a continent, not an island or a group of islands. Since Europeans believed there were only three continents in the world, this land must be a part of the Asian continent.

Ferdinand and Isabella were also pleased to hear Amerigo could determine longitude accurately. They wanted him to make another voyage for them, but he became ill again. He returned to Seville, where Maria took care of him. Gradually his fever disappeared.

One day while he was still resting, a messenger arrived from King Manuel of Portugal. The messenger told Amerigo the king wanted him to come to Lisbon for a talk. Amerigo knew he'd strayed into Portuguese territory on his voyage, but he wondered if the Portuguese knew it.

In 1494, the Treaty of Tordesillas had given Spain all the territory to the west of a certain line of longitude. Portugal was to have any land lying to the east of the line. It wasn't until Amerigo learned how to figure out longitude on his voyage that he discovered he was in Portuguese land.

He told King Manuel's messenger he'd entered the king's territory by mistake and begged his pardon. The messenger said the king wasn't angry. He wanted Amerigo to sail to the Indies for Portugal. At first, Amerigo said no, but the Portuguese king wouldn't give up. He sent another messenger, and finally Amerigo decided to go and hear what the king had to say.

As soon as his meeting with King Manuel began, Amerigo learned spies had told the king of Amerigo's new way of calculating longitude. King Manuel told Amerigo that, skillful as his navigators were, none of them could determine longitude accurately. He asked if Amerigo would sail to the Indies and mark the boundaries of Portuguese territory.

Amerigo still wanted to find the Cape of Catigara that Ptolemy spoke of and the part of Asia that Marco Polo had described. He knew he had to go through Portuguese territory to get there. Since it was common practice for explorers to work for different kings, and Amerigo had no business left in Seville and no official post, he decided to sail under the Portuguese flag.

His three-caravel expedition left Lisbon on May 10, 1501. Before crossing the Ocean Sea, they sailed farther down the coast of Africa than Amerigo's last expedition had. They went all the way to Dakar, where the African continent juts farthest out into the Ocean Sea. Here the distance across the sea would be shortest.

Perhaps the ships could make the trip in as little as three weeks. The Portuguese caravels were faster, stronger, and easier to handle than Spain's. And Portuguese sailors had found ways of obeying orders quickly. They hung garlic on the right side of the ship and onions on the left so they never had to stop and think which side was which when the captain shouted an order. They seemed to love sailing.

While the ships were in Dakar taking on fresh supplies, Amerigo measured the movements of the stars and their angles against the horizon. He made a discovery that amazed him. The earth was 27,000 Roman miles in circumference, not 22,500 miles as Toscanelli thought. Certainly not 20,400 miles as Columbus thought.

Then a Portuguese expedition on its way north sailed into port. The ships had gone around the southern tip of Africa, then east to the Indies, and were coming back to Europe. None of the places they described sounded anything like what Amerigo had seen on his voyage to the Indies. Amerigo began to wonder if he'd really been in the Indies at all.

Amerigo's expedition finally left Dakar, sailing south and then west into the worst weather he'd ever seen. The wind whipped the waves and howled through the rigging of the sails. Day followed stormy day, and there wasn't a single calm night.

Amerigo reassured the sailors they were moving toward the Indies even though they were sailing in a zigzag pattern. He showed the men his methods of navigation.   They understood little about using the astrolabe and almost nothing of his way of determining longitude.   But their fears were calmed by Amerigo's knowledge.

As the trip went on and on, the food supply dwindled. The ships ran out of meat first, then wood for the fire. They ate the last of the cheese and olives. After that, all that was left was raw flour. Amerigo began to wonder if they would ever make land.

While Amerigo and Columbus sailed in search of a western route to the Indies, the Portuguese explorer Vasco da Gama reached India by sailing east. He is shown here meeting with a local ruler in Calicut, India.

VII
An Amazing Discovery

On August 15, after the ships had been at sea 64 days, a lookout finally spotted land. Using his quadrant, Amerigo figured they were about 5½ degrees south of the equator. Amerigo's letters don't tell us how the explorers found food, but perhaps they shot birds or gathered fruit. Bananas, pineapples, and papaya grew wild in the area.

At any rate, they sailed north to a place they named Cape Saint Rocco (Cabo São Roque), after the saint who had been born on that day, August 16. They were close to the southernmost point of Amerigo's last voyage. Satisfied they hadn't missed Catigara, they turned and headed south against the northerly current.

After a day of struggling and zigzag sailing, the ships were miles farther south, and the current was weakening. Soon they passed it altogether. Now

Amerigo's love of observing the stars led to his realization that he had not traveled to the Indies at all, but had reached another continent.

there was nothing to stop them from reaching the Cape of Catigara. Whenever they found a cape, bay, or river, they gave it the name of the saint whose birthday it was that day.

Finally they were eight degrees south of the equator, just where Ptolemy said the Cape of Catigara was. All they had to do was round this cape to be in the Indies of Marco Polo, Amerigo thought.

Then he read in his almanac that there would be

a conjunction of the moon with Mars just a few days later. This would be a good time to determine their longitude. Since it was easier to do this on dry land than on shipboard, they decided to wait on the cape until the conjunction occurred.

When it happened, Amerigo calculated their distance from Europe. He realized they were nowhere near Catigara because they weren't in the Indies at all. Asia would have to cover half the globe to extend this far east. Marco Polo had said the continent was huge, but not that huge. Amerigo's expedition had to be on the coast of another continent Europeans knew nothing about.

For some time, Amerigo had been wondering if he were really in Asia. Everything here was so different from the descriptions of Marco Polo and the Portuguese who had sailed to Asia by way of Africa. He checked his figures again. There could be no mistake. The explorers had found a fourth continent. The belief that the world was made up of only Europe, Africa and Asia was wrong.

Amerigo didn't tell the sailors right away. Perhaps he thought they might be frightened at being in an entirely unknown place. They named the cape Saint Augustine and sailed on.

They made many landfalls along the way and saw many people. Because he knew he wasn't in Asia, Amerigo was no longer surprised that they were different from Asians. (In his letters, he never again referred to them as "Indians.") He described the people later in a letter to Il Popolano. "They are . . . well proportioned in body, with black hair and little or no beard. The men are in the habit of decorating their lips and cheeks with bones and stones which they suspend from holes bored in them. I have seen some of them with three, seven, and even as many as nine holes, filled with white or green alabaster— a . . . custom which they follow in order . . . to make themselves appear fierce. . . ."

These people, probably of the Tupinambá tribe, were friendly, however. The explorers ate and slept in their villages and stretched out on their hammocks at the siesta hour. Amerigo found the hammocks much more comfortable than sleeping on the ground with a blanket. He was impressed with the native people's houses too. "For people who have no iron or any metal, one can call their houses truly miraculous . . . I have seen habitations which are 220 paces long and 30 wide, ingeniously made."

Amerigo was fascinated with the native people's customs. "They did not seem to have religion or law of any kind, nor any king, each one being the master of himself." Although they had frequent wars, they didn't fight over land or possessions. Instead, they said they fought "to avenge the murder of their ancestors," Amerigo wrote.

He learned these people treated prisoners like the Caribs to the north did. "They eat them and consider them very delicious food . . . . Human flesh, having been salted, was hung from the beams of the dwellings.

They were greatly astonished that we did not eat our enemies. . . ."

Amerigo approved of the rest of the local food. Besides fruits and a great variety of fish, they enjoyed crabs, oysters, lobsters, and turtles. And they told Amerigo they had gold and other metals. Amerigo didn't see any, so he doubted it. "I am one of those who, like Saint Thomas, are slow to believe. Time will tell all," his letter to Il Popolano said.

The expedition sailed farther and farther south. On November 1, All Saints Day, the explorers discovered a bay and named it All Saints Bay. Amerigo continued to find the coast full of wonders. "Who could count the wild animals, the abundance of lions and cats, not those of Spain any longer, but of the Southern Hemisphere?" he wrote. "All the wolves, baboons, monkeys of many kinds, some of them so large. We saw more wild animals such as boars, goats, deer and rabbits than could ever have entered the ark of Noah."

They sailed south for 10 months, wandering over sea and land. Amerigo was impressed with the health of the people. "If they chance to fall sick, they cure themselves immediately with the juice of herbs," he wrote. "They do not know how to keep time in days, months and years, but reckon time by lunar months. When they wish to demonstrate something involving time, they do it by placing one pebble for each lunar month on the ground." One old man, using pebbles, told Amerigo that he was 132 years old. These may have been the Guaraní people, who then lived on the southern coast of what is now Brazil.

On February 15, 1502, the explorers came to a place where the shoreline veered west. Amerigo took careful bearings and told the ship captains they had come to the edge of Spanish territory. The captains wanted to continue following the coast, but they were Portuguese and might get into trouble if they explored Spanish territory. They left it to Amerigo to decide.

Amerigo couldn't keep the truth from them any longer. They weren't on the coast of Asia, he said, but on a new continent. By sailing around the tip of this continent, they would find another sea. Asia would lie beyond that sea. There they would find the Indies of Marco Polo.

No one knows what the captain and crew said when Amerigo told them this, but they must have been astonished. They discussed it for a long time. Finally they decided to continue going south. They would sail quickly, making stops only when they had to find food or repair the ships. They wouldn't explore the land because it belonged to Spain.

Before setting sail, the men put up a marking stone to show the end of Portuguese territory. Then they sailed past what is now Uruguay and down the coast of Argentina. At 50 degrees south latitude, the crew named a port after Saint Julian. They were farther south than the Portuguese had gone when they rounded the tip of Africa. The explorers must have wondered if the new continent would ever end.

It was April now, autumn in the Southern Hemisphere. They were so close to the South Pole that the nights lasted 15 hours. Even the days seemed like night because dark clouds shut out the sunlight. They saw no more harbors, and the cold was intense.

Huge gray waves loomed before them. The ship, pushed by fierce winds, rose up a wave, hit the crest with a bump, and raced down the other side. Another wave came at them. No sooner were they down its other side than still another wave loomed up. The ship bucked under the explorers' feet like a frightened horse.

The captain shouted orders, trying to change course, but the ship raced south. Then some brave sailors, fighting gale winds that threatened to blow them from the deck, managed to change the ship's direction from south to east. The ship sped east until they came to a place calm enough to turn northwest. They sped in that direction until the rocky coast reappeared, then turned the ship east again and went far enough out to sea to turn northwest once more. In this way, the skillful Portuguese sailors zigzagged away from the storm. Then, exhausted, they headed northeast for Africa.

Amerigo's expedition had gone all the way to five degrees south latitude. When they finally made it across the sea, one of the ships was so damaged that the sailors burned it. The explorers rested on the African coast and arrived in Lisbon in September 1502. They had outrun the storm, and Amerigo had news that would astonish the world.

VIII
A New World

As soon as Amerigo arrived in Lisbon, he told King Manuel about the long coastline he had explored. He wrote to Il Popolano too. Amerigo told both of them that the coast was part of a new continent unknown to Europeans. History doesn't tell us what King Manuel replied, but he must have been astounded. Like everyone else, he thought Amerigo and Columbus had been in Asia exploring the Indies.

Amerigo said Asia was much farther west, and another ocean must lie between it and the continent that Amerigo had visited. He gave the king a map of the coast and his records of the trip. In his letter to Il Popolano, Amerigo said he would send more information when the king returned his papers. The records, he said, "will bring me some fame after my death."

King Manuel usually kept facts about Portuguese

explorations secret, but he couldn't keep this news quiet. In a short time, a Portuguese map showing the new continent with a sea separating it from Asia circulated in Lisbon and then in Spain.

King Manuel realized he had to establish Portuguese colonies on the new continent if he wanted to hold onto his territory there. He asked Amerigo to sail again under the Portuguese flag. Since Amerigo wanted another chance to find a way around the new continent to the real Indies, he agreed to go.

On May 10, 1503, Amerigo sailed as captain of a ship in a six-ship expedition. In the middle of the Ocean Sea, the expedition ran into a terrible storm. Amerigo's ship became separated from the others. After eight days, he found one other ship. Its captain told him the other four had been lost.

Without the men and supplies from the other four ships, it would be difficult to build and stock a fort for the colonists on the new coast. Amerigo probably considered returning to Portugal, but they were more than halfway to the new continent. He decided to continue the voyage west.

The two ships reached the place Amerigo had named All Saints Bay on his last voyage. There was little time to explore. The expedition had lost so many men at sea, the 24 remaining colonists needed the crewmen to help build their fort. The expedition made only a short trip of exploration south, then turned around and sailed to a cape they named Cabo Frio (Cold Cape). There the men built a fort.

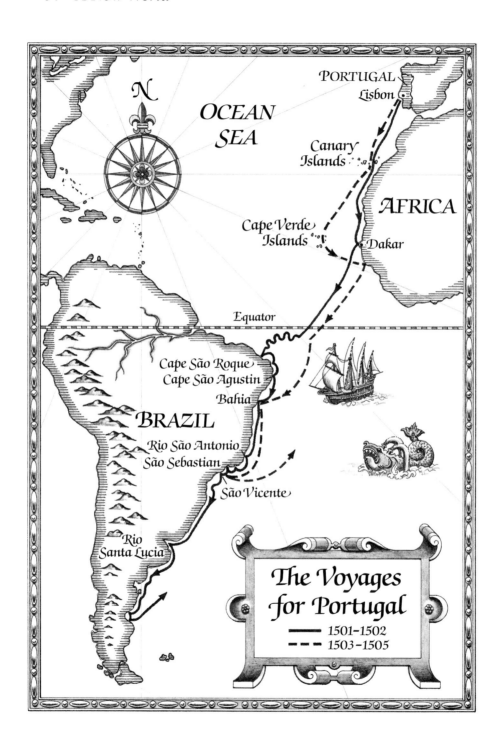

N

*OCEAN
SEA*

PORTUGAL
Lisbon

Canary
Islands

AFRICA

Cape Verde
Islands

Dakar

Equator

Cape São Roque
Cape São Agustin
Bahia

BRAZIL

Rio São Antonio
São Sebastian

São Vicente

Rio
Santa Lucia

The Voyages
for Portugal

——— 1501–1502
- - - - 1503–1505

When it was finished, Amerigo loaded the ships with logs from Brazil trees, which grew everywhere. He also took cassia, a bark used as a medicine and as a spice. Although he would have loved sailing around this continent to the Indies, too many of the necessary provisions and men had gone down with the four lost ships. Amerigo sailed back to Portugal, leaving the colonists with provisions for six months.

The Portuguese flocked to greet the seamen when they reached Lisbon in June of 1505. As before, Amerigo gave the king a report of the voyage and lent him his records of the trip. Then he set out for Spain.

He reached home at the end of 1505 and learned that Queen Isabella was dead and King Ferdinand was ruling Spain. The king invited him to court and sent him a large amount of money for travel expenses.

On his way to court, Amerigo visited Columbus and found the explorer weary and old-looking. Columbus was resentful because King Ferdinand had given him only a fraction of the properties and titles he had promised.

He didn't believe Amerigo's news of a new continent, for he was certain the new lands were part of Asia. The two old friends didn't argue about it, however. Amerigo promised he would ask the king to give Columbus what he owed him. He would also take a letter to Columbus's son Diego on his way.

When Amerigo arrived at court, he spoke to King Ferdinand about Columbus. But the king only wanted to talk about his territory on the new continent. The king said Spanish ships were running aground on unfamiliar shores and sinking in unknown seas. A master map of the new continent must be made, and he needed Amerigo's help. Would Amerigo become a Spanish citizen and be the king's adviser?

Amerigo accepted Spanish citizenship and set to work mapping King Ferdinand's lands in the New World. As the king's adviser, he listened to problems about governing the colonies. He met with Spanish sea captains and decided what exploration should be done next.

On March 22, 1508, the king honored him again. "For his good service," Ferdinand made Amerigo Pilot Major of Spain. There had never been such a post in Spain before. Amerigo was to gather together the most skillful pilots "to settle up and draw a master map of all the lands and islands . . . to be known as the royal chart. . . ." Any pilot who used a chart not drawn by Amerigo would be fined. Anyone sailing in the Indies who found something not already on the master chart had to report it to the pilot major.

Amerigo was also to head a university of mariners. Town criers in all the cities and hamlets of Spain read a proclamation to the roll of drums. Amerigo Vespucci would teach pilots how to use the quadrant and the astrolabe, the proclamation said. He would test them and give them certificates to sail. Any pilot setting out without a certificate would be declared unfit to sail for a period of time and fined.

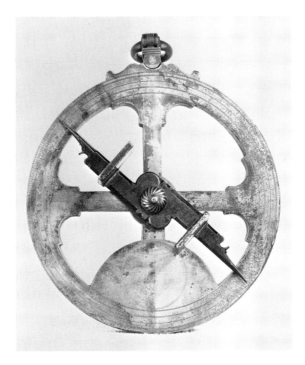

Unlike many sailors of the time, Amerigo was skilled in the use of the mariner's astrolabe.

Amerigo's house in Seville became the university where seamen studied until they learned enough to get their certificates. His nephew Giovanni helped him run the school and made maps there.

Amerigo must have enjoyed putting on the master chart the new information Spanish pilots and captains brought in. He was doing what he loved most — finding out about the world as it was, not as it had been imagined.

As pilot major, Amerigo also instructed ships' outfitters what to supply the colonists. He helped write laws to prevent stealing and smuggling. He had all Spanish ships plated with lead to withstand storms and the wood worms that ate ships' hulls.

Amerigo was probably disappointed that he couldn't teach all the pilots his method of determining longitude. Most of them didn't know enough astronomy to tell one planet from another. The few who did had trouble measuring the distance between the planets and the moon. Some couldn't do the math required to translate time into miles accurately.

During his four years as pilot major, Amerigo suffered an occasional attack of chills and fever, undoubtedly from malaria. Then one cold day in February, when he was 58, Amerigo came down with an especially bad attack. No one in Europe knew the bark of the cinchona tree, which Amerigo had seen in Venezuela and Brazil, contained quinine, a medicine that could help him. Maria and Giovanni could only watch helplessly as Amerigo got sicker. On February 22, 1512, he died.

His death was a great loss to Spain. But a great gift that he left it was the school of navigation, which Giovanni kept going. A new generation of seamen was trained there. They continued Spain's exploration of what had come to be called the "New World."

Amerigo, like many Florentines, hoped his name would live after him. But he would have been astonished at what a great honor it received after his death. He would have been shocked when his name was later dishonored and forgotten.

Afterword:
The Naming
of America

In 1507, a letter supposedly written to Il Popolano by Amerigo Vespucci, along with a map of the regions Amerigo visited, reached a small monastery in the mountains of France. The monks there were about to write a geography book based on Ptolemy's map. When they saw the new map and Amerigo's letter, they changed their minds. They wrote a geography book based on the astounding news of a fourth continent.

One of the monks, Martin Waldseemüller, drew a map for the book and printed the name "America" on what is now known as South America. One of the other monks wrote in the book, "It is fitting that this fourth part of the world, inasmuch as Americus [Latin for Amerigo] discovered it, be called . . . America."

The monks had a printing press, so they were able to make many copies of the book, which then circulated

Part of Martin Waldseemüller's map of 1507, which was the first map to use the name America. The way the Americas are drawn is based on information from letters allegedly written by Amerigo.

throughout Europe. In 1522, after Waldseemüller and Amerigo had both died, the map was reprinted in Germany. After that, almost all maps of the world placed the name America on the central and southern part of the New World. In 1538, the name was

A drawing of Amerigo, next to a globe showing the fourth continent, is featured at the top of Waldseemüller's map.

placed on the northern part also. Amerigo's original maps were lost.

Years later, after the Spanish had come to realize the great size and value of the New World, they began to regret their treatment of Columbus. Bartolomé de Las Casas, a Spanish priest who worked among the "Indians" (as Native Americans were still called), thought Vespucci must be responsible for Spain's neglect of Columbus. He wrote a book saying that Amerigo made up the 1497 voyage so he could claim he reached the new continent before Columbus (who first saw it in 1498). Las Casas said Amerigo stole Columbus's glory by naming the New World after himself. He cited mistakes in a letter of Amerigo's that told about the 1497 voyage. What Las Casas didn't know was that this letter (supposedly to Amerigo's friend Piero Soderini) and others that circulated throughout Europe with Amerigo's signature were not written by him.

These letters borrowed freely from Amerigo's real letters, but placed areas Amerigo had actually visited at the wrong latitudes and said they occurred at impossible times. They made up incidents designed to whet the reader's appetite for sensational stories. The Soderini letter described the nakedness of the women and their supposedly outrageous behavior toward men. One said Amerigo witnessed one of his sailors being eaten by cannibals. These forged letters were printed and sold throughout Europe.

Later historians quoted Las Casas, and most people came to believe Amerigo was a liar. Between 1825 and 1837, a Spanish historian, Martin de Navarrete, published a famous collection of documents relating to the discovery of America. It has been a source book for scholars ever since.

De Navarrete repeated the mistakes of Las Casas and made many of his own about Amerigo. These mistakes were quoted by others. People began to wonder if Amerigo had made any voyages at all. Some Americans thought Amerigo was nothing but a Seville businessman who wrote lying boasts about voyages he never took. Many American history books stopped mentioning his name.

Then, in the late 19th century, scholars such as Henry Harrisse took a new look at Amerigo's letters and at government records. De Navarrete had said the Spanish Ledger of Fleet Expenses showed Amerigo was in Seville during 1497 outfitting ships for Columbus and couldn't have made the 1497 voyage. Harrisse pointed out that mention of Amerigo's name in the records stopped in 1496 and didn't resume until 1505. Amerigo could have gone on that voyage and the other three as well.

Other scholars looked at a map made by Juan de la Cosa—a pilot who had sailed with both Amerigo and Columbus—in 1500. On it, the coastline of North America is shown as far north as Cape Hatteras in North Carolina. Since neither de la Cosa nor anyone else claimed to have sailed this coast before 1500, it's likely that the map was based on Amerigo's trip of 1497.

This illustration, from a history of exploration published in 1594, recognizes the contributions of both Amerigo and Columbus. Later historians were not as kind to Amerigo.

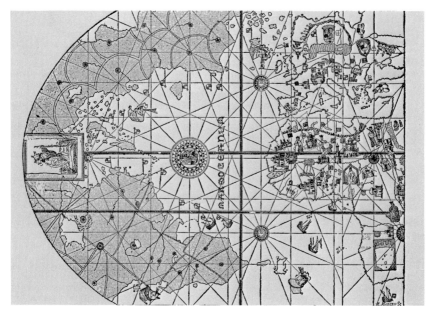

Juan de la Cosa made this map, based on his travels with Amerigo and Columbus, in 1500.

The map also shows Florida realistically as a peninsula and Cuba as an island. This information must have come from Amerigo's 1497 trip. Columbus's maps still showed Cuba as part of mainland China and didn't show Florida at all.

The forged Soderini letter, which told of the 1497 voyage, contains some factual information, such as its accurate description of Cape Hatteras. It also gives the correct latitude of Saint Augustine on the Brazilian coast (information given in no other document of the time). It's also the only letter that mentions Amerigo's last voyage for Portugal. It shows a good knowledge of the land around Cabo Frio. And there really was a colony there. In 1511, a Portuguese captain wrote in his ship's log book that he had "visited Cabo Frio, the colony Amerigo Vespucci started." The log book still exists in Portugal.

Historians now think someone who knew Amerigo wrote the letter. This would account for the fact that some of its information is correct.

Although some historians still doubt Amerigo made a voyage in 1497, others now believe that Amerigo did indeed make the other three (in 1499, 1501, and 1503). They give him credit for inventing the Method of Lunar Distances for finding longitude. Even though the difficulty of this method made it too hard for many sea captains to use, outstanding navigators like Captain Cook, the first European to see Hawaii and Australia, used it. (Most captains were unable to figure their longitude at sea until the chronometer was invented in 1714.)

Historians praise Amerigo for figuring out the true circumference of the earth (within 50 miles) at a time when other geographers were thousands of miles off the true figure. Some historians believe he sailed almost the entire coast of Central and South America and some of the coast of North America.

If naming the New World had been left to Amerigo, he probably would have named it after Columbus. He respected Columbus's skill and courage in leading Europeans across the Ocean Sea and remained a good friend of the explorer and his sons. Amerigo never put the name America on his maps, nor did his nephew Giovanni put the name on the maps he made.

Lettera di Amerigo vespucci delle isole nuouamente trouate in quattro suoi viaggi.

The first page of an Italian edition of the *Four Voyages*, the forged letters supposedly written by Amerigo to Piero Soderini. The title means "Letters by Amerigo Vespucci about Islands Newly Discovered in his Four Voyages."

Amerigo's greatest achievement was realizing that the coast he and Columbus explored was part of a new continent. Most explorers of the time saw what legend and the beliefs of the Middle Ages told them to expect. Amerigo, too well educated and skeptical to accept the legends of his time as fact, saw what was really there. Having seen a fourth continent, he told the world about it.

The light Amerigo shed on world geography helped put an end to the dark ages of history when superstition counted for more than knowledge. Amerigo Vespucci was a voyager to be remembered.

Bibliography

Arciniegas, German. *Amerigo and the New World*. New York: Alfred A. Knopf, Inc., 1955.

Brophy, Patrick. *Sailing Ships*. London: The Hamlyn Publishing Group Ltd., 1974.

Hale, John, et al. *Age of Exploration*. New York: Time Inc., 1966.

Laguarda Trias, Rolando A. *El hallazgo del Rio de la Plata por Amerigo Vespucci*. Montivideo, Uruguay: Academia Nacional de Letras, 1982.

Landstrom, Bjorn. *Bold Voyages and Great Explorers*. Garden City, New York: Doubleday and Company, Inc., 1964.

Pohl, Frederick. *Amerigo Vespucci, Pilot Major*. New York: Columbia University Press, 1944.

Vespucci, Amerigo. *Lettere di Viaggio*. A Cura di Luciano Formisano. Milan: Arnoldo Mondadori Editore, 1985.

Index